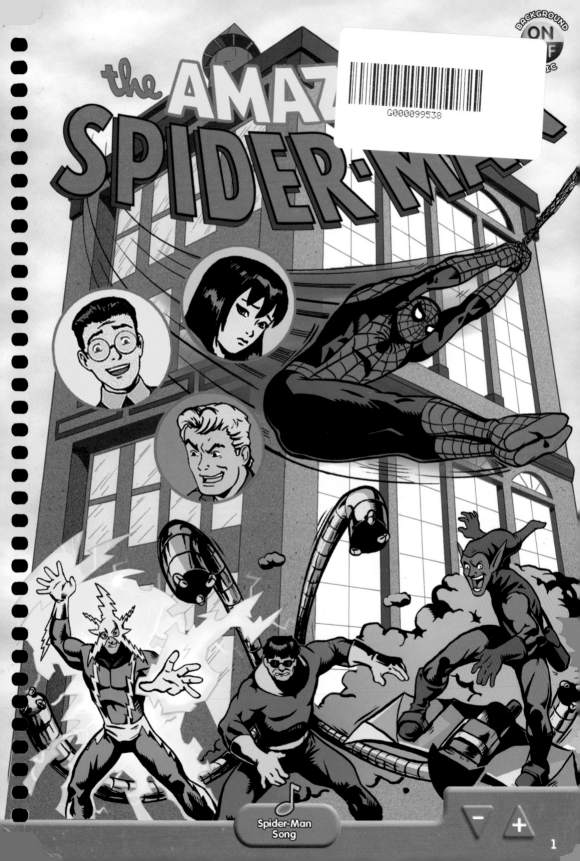

Spider-Man
Song

↪ Like heroes? Well, here's a story about one who's just a little bit... different.

• Building words   • Letter names and sounds

Read to me

It all starts in New York City with a smart, shy guy named Peter Parker. The kids in Peter's class call him names.

↱ The **setting**: science class. ↱ Watch closely as a small **spider** drops from the machine onto Peter's hand! CHOMP!

GO

STOP

• Animal classification • Compare and contrast

Read to me

Bird-dropping Spider

Redback Spider

Flower Spider

Common House Spider

St. Andrew's Cross Spider

Phidippus Jumping Spider

Bolas Spider

Net-casting Spider

Mexican Red Knee Tarantula

Funnel-web Spider

Peter starts to feel... different.

Spider-power flows through him, changing him into...

1 SPIDER-SENSE

A CAR'S COMING! I CAN FEEL IT!

2 SPIDER-GRIP

3 SPIDER-ACROBATICS

4 SPIDER-STRENGTH

• **Synonyms and antonyms**   • **Critical thinking**

Read to me

5 SPIDER-WEBBING

Matching
GAME

repeat

WITH THESE NEW POWERS, I CAN DO ANYTHING!

GO

APARTMENT

MALL

BANK

GENIUS

STOP

Read to me

• Letter identification in words
• Recognizing ordinal numbers

Three of New York City's meanest **crooks** are meeting. Calling themselves "Triple Trouble," **evil** Electro, Green Goblin and Doctor Octopus plan to chase our hero out of town.

Name: Electro
Power: Shoots electricity
Gear: None
History: Former Electrician

GO

• Outlining skills

Read to me

STOP

Name: Doctor Octopus

Power: Uses steel arms for super strength and climbing

Gear: Four steel tentacles help him travel and spin quickly

History: Former scientist

Name: The Green Goblin

Power: Superhuman strength, really smart, heals quickly

Gear: Flying Goblin Glider, pumpkin bombs, and electrical gloves

History: Former president of Osborn Industries

"We must get rid of this Spider-Man!" Doctor Octopus says. "Yes, as fast as **lightning**!" Electro says. "Anytime! Anywhere! I'll be there, flying through the air!" Green Goblin yells.

DAILY ✦ BUGLE™
NEW YORK'S FINEST DAILY NEWSPAPER

① → 'Triple Trouble' Plan to Crush
Spider-Man!

② → Last night the Bugle received a note from the dangerous criminals known as Triple Trouble. It says:

③ → Dear People of New York,

It's a sad day for this old city when a man **disguised** as a spider can scare our hardworking crooks.

④ → This city is ours — every tall building and every dirty street.

⑤ → Spider-Man, you cannot run. You cannot hide. So come out and fight!

GO

STOP

Read to me

• Matching pictures and words   • Parts of speech

Spider-Man doesn't waste any time – the people of the city are in danger!

He searches for his **enemies** high above the city streets.

Spider-Man sees Electro first and chases him into an **alley**. Electro laughs, spins around, and shoots lightning at Spider-Man.

ZAAP!

GO

COMPOUND WORDS

Basketball

Teacup

Skateboard

Hamburger

Read to me

• Matching pictures and words   • Electricity properties

STOP

Think fast, Spidey, and remember that lightning will go right to anything metal!

ONE DOWN, TWO TO GO!

Fishbowl   Popcorn

Doghouse   Toothbrush

Watermelon   Raincoat

WHOOSH! What's that? **Something** strange **flying** high above the city!

SPROING! Spider-Man jumps closer to get a better look. It's the Green Goblin! The **battle** begins...

GO

STOP

Read to me

• Match oral and printed words   • Blends and diagraphs

Spidey kicks the **glider**! Goblin falls! Then Spidey drops down to **capture** him!

↪ Now Spider-Man must face his most dangerous enemy, the evil Doctor Octopus.

↪ He follows his spider-sense to an old warehouse where the Doctor is waiting.

GO

• Understanding events and characters

Read to me

Spider-Man bravely leaps at the Doctor.
The mad scientist's metal arms catch
Spider-Man and hold him in the air. Oh no!

Doctor Octopus is strong, but he's no match for Spider-Man's wit.

• Long vowel sounds   • Short vowel sounds

Looks like Peter can handle those bullies just fine. Wouldn't *you* if you had spider-powers?

• Matching   • Sequencing   Read to me   Spider-Man Song

GO

STOP

SETTING

The Train Station!

The Brooklyn Bridge!

The Old Factory!

CHARACTER

Sandman!

Spider-webbing!

Mysterio!

Rhino!

EVENT

Spider-strength!

Spider-acrobatics!

MY STORY!

Create a Story
GAME

repeat

Check out these other
LeapPad™ books
for 1st Grade!

1st Grade

© Disney/Pixar

TM & © Hanna-Barbera
TM & © Cartoon Network (S02)

Dr. Seuss properties™ & © 2004 Dr. Seuss
Enterprises, L.P. All Rights Reserved

2nd Grade

Is your child ready for the 2nd grade?

Dr. Seuss properties™ & © 2004 Dr. Seuss
Enterprises, L.P. All Rights Reserved

TM & © Hanna-Barbera
TM & © Cartoon Network (S02)

© 2003 Viacom International Inc.
Created by Stephen Hillenburg

The LeapPad Library
includes over 60 books from
Pre-K to 5th Grade!
Visit **www.leapfrog.com** to learn more!

All books may
not be available
in all markets.
Actual covers may vary.